LAB LOGISTICS AND SAFETY

FIRE AND ICE!

MEASURING TEMPERATURES IN THE LAB

JILL SHERMAN

PowerKiDS
press

New York

Published in 2021 by The Rosen Publishing Group, Inc.
29 East 21st Street, New York, NY 10010

First Edition

Editor: Jane Katirgis
Book Design: Reann Nye

Photo Credits: Cover jcphoto/iStock/Getty Images Plus/Getty Images; series art Triff/Shutterstock.com; p. 5 hxdbzxy/Darrin Klimek/DigitalVision/Getty Images; p. 7 Rawpixel.com/Shutterstock.com; p. 9 Science & Society Picture Library/SSPL/Getty Images; p. 11 Joyseulay/Shutterstock.com; p. 12 Cathetus/Shutterstock.com; p. 13 Monkey Business Images/Shutterstock.com; p. 15 Michael Rolands/iStock/Getty Images Plus/Getty Images; p. 17 P-fotography/Shutterstock.com; p. 19 Hero Images/Getty Images; p. 21 wavebreakmedia/Shutterstock.com; p. 22 lammotos/Shutterstock.com.

Library of Congress Cataloging-in-Publication Data

Names: Sherman, Jill, author.
Title: Fire and ice! : measuring temperatures in the lab / Jill Sherman.
Other titles: Measuring temperatures in the lab
Description: New York : PowerKids Press, [2021] | Series: Lab logistics and safety | Includes index. | Summary: "Measuring the temperature of different types of matter is a key component of many different branches of science, especially chemistry. However, for a long time, scientists could only tell if something was hot or cold and didn't have a way to tell precisely hot or how cold that thing was. Today, we use thermometers in the Fahrenheit, Celsius, and Kelvin scales to measure temperature. Diagrams and fact boxes help readers understand the practical uses of each scale and how to safely measure temperature in the lab"– Provided by publisher.
Identifiers: LCCN 2019032583 | ISBN 9781725310308 (paperback) | ISBN 9781725310322 (library binding) | ISBN 9781725310315 (6 pack) | ISBN 9781725310339 (ebook)
Subjects: LCSH: Temperature measurements–Juvenile literature. | Thermometers–Juvenile literature. | Science rooms and equipment–Juvenile literature. | Science–Study and teaching–Juvenile literature. | Laboratories–Safety measures–Juvenile literature.
Classification: LCC QC271.4 .S446 2020 | DDC 536/.50287–dc23
LC record available at https://lccn.loc.gov/2019032583

Manufactured in the United States of America

CPSIA Compliance Information: Batch #CSPK20. For Further Information contact Rosen Publishing, New York, New York at 1-800-237-9932.

CONTENTS

TAKING TEMPERATURE

Temperature can be a very important thing when you're doing experiments in the lab. How hot or cold something is can have a big effect on an experiment, or it can be a result from your experiment. Either way, temperature is an important data point you can measure. To measure temperature, you use an instrument called a thermometer.

Experiments might include taking the temperature of chemicals under different conditions. You might check air temperatures, or you might track a person's body temperature. It's important to be safe and careful when working in the lab, especially when you're dealing with temperature **extremes**!

IN THE LAB!

A healthy human body temperature is about 98.6°Fahrenheit (37°Celsius). If a person's temperature is much higher, it means something is wrong. The person probably has a fever.

If your temperature is too high, you may have to visit your doctor to help you get well.

WORKING IN A LAB

Working in a science lab can be a lot of fun, but it's important to remember to be careful. Always follow the lab **procedures**.

Working in a lab is all about discovery and learning. Each experiment is meant to test a **hypothesis**. If you vary from the procedure, you may not get exact results, and all your work could be wasted.

Following lab procedure also helps keep you and your lab partner safe. The lab isn't a place for joking around. Stay focused on the experiment and you'll be on your way to an enjoyable (and productive) lab experience.

Check your notes to be sure you're following the correct procedure during an experiment.

DEGREES OF MEASUREMENT

Early scientists knew that objects could be hot or cold. But to study temperatures in the lab, scientists needed a way to measure them in a **precise** way. They imagined a ruler that measured levels of hot and cold.

When some **substances** are heated, they expand, or take up more space. When they're cooled, they contract, or take up less space. So, if placed in a narrow tube, one of these substances will take up more space in the tube as it's heated, making its level rise. This is how the first thermometers were invented. Today, there are many kinds of **accurate** thermometers.

IN THE LAB!

There are a number of temperature scales, but the most common are Fahrenheit and Celsius. Each scale measures temperature in degrees. Most scientists use Celsius for measurements.

This alcohol thermometer was used in the 18th century.

9

CHOOSING A THERMOMETER

In the lab, you want to choose the right tool for the job. Which thermometer is best for your experiment?

One thing to consider is the scale. You probably won't be measuring something that's very, very hot or very, very cold, but some scales and thermometers are better for that than others. Some thermometers are better for air temperature or liquids. Others measure body temperature.

A thermometer used to measure body temperature has a small range, from about 95°F (35°C) to 107.6°F (42°C). On the other hand, an outdoor thermometer that measures air temperature has a larger range, from about -30°F (-34.4°C) to 120°F (49°C).

IN THE LAB!

How do we know the temperatures of objects in space? Scientists from the National Aeronautics and Space Administration (NASA) use special infrared thermometers. All objects glow with a kind of light called infrared light. The brightness of the infrared light shows its temperature.

This infrared thermometer is showing which parts of a building are warm and which are cold. What could that information be used for?

LAB SAFETY

Safety is always important when working in a lab. Wear proper protective gear, such as gloves and safety goggles.

Always clean a thermometer before using it. Rinse it with **deionized water** and then dry it completely. You don't want to **contaminate** the substance you're measuring or cause a dangerous chemical change.

Some thermometers have liquid in them. The liquid might be alcohol or an element called mercury. Take care when using a mercury thermometer. Mercury is toxic and dangerous to your health. If a thermometer breaks, don't touch the mercury. Tell an adult, who will clean it up safely.

IN THE LAB!

Mercury thermometers are very popular. They are highly accurate and easy to read. Also, mercury is a metal, and it reacts quickly to changes in temperature.

Safety goggles will prevent chemicals from splashing into your eyes.

13

SETTING UP YOUR THERMOMETER

When taking a temperature reading in a lab, it's best not to hold on to the thermometer or the container of whatever you're measuring. The warmth from your hands could change the temperature.

If possible, use a ring stand and a **clamp** to hold your thermometer. The clamp keeps the thermometer suspended in the material you're measuring. This way, the thermometer doesn't touch the sides or bottom of the container. This will give you the most accurate reading.

Also, since you don't need to touch the thermometer, you're less likely to accidentally spill any liquid or break your equipment.

Following lab procedure helps you do safe and accurate testing.

MADE IN UK

76 MM.

REACHING EQUILIBRIUM

Thermal, or heat, energy always flows from warm objects to cooler ones. The energy leaves the warm object, making it cooler, and the cool object takes on that energy. When the two objects are the same temperature, they've reached a state of **equilibrium**. No more energy is exchanged.

Once the thermometer is set up, don't read the measurement immediately. Allow the thermometer time to warm or cool to the surrounding temperature. When the measurement stops moving, the thermometer's temperature reading should be the same as whatever you are measuring. It's reached equilibrium. You have your reading.

IN THE LAB!

The science of heat and energy is called thermodynamics. There are three main scientific laws of thermodynamics. First, energy can't be created or destroyed. Second, thermal energy always flows from a warmer object to a cooler one. Third, it's impossible for an object to have no thermal energy.

Heat always flows from warm areas to cool ones. If you pour a cold cup of water on a hot day, the water will grow warmer even as it cools down the area around it.

CONVERTING TEMPERATURES

Once you have your temperature measurements, you may want to compare them to other measurements. Always check that the temperature scales you're using match. If your measurements are in Fahrenheit but you want to compare them to Celsius measurements, you'll need to convert the measurements.

On the Fahrenheit scale, the freezing and boiling points of water are 180 degrees apart. Water freezes at 32°F and water boils at 212°F. In Celsius, the freezing point of water is 0°C. The boiling point is 100°C.

To convert from Celsius to Fahrenheit, multiply by 1.8 and add 32. Do the reverse for Fahrenheit to Celsius: subtract 32, then divide by 1.8.

IN THE LAB!

Digital thermometers don't use mercury or alcohol. They use a digital **thermistor**. A thermistor's resistance changes when temperature changes. A small computer measures this change, and the thermometer shows the temperature on an easy-to-read screen.

Using math, you can convert temperatures from one scale to another. The Kelvin scale is another scale often used by scientists.

REPEATED MEASURES

Good scientists don't take just one measurement. Once they complete their experiment, they will start over and do it again. This helps them to gather more data and improve accuracy.

Maybe in your first experiment, you measured something at a temperature of 25°F (-3.9°C). But in your other same experiments, you measured it at 33°F (0.6°C), 34°F (1.1°C), and 33°F (0.6°C). You would know that something went wrong the first time or changed in the other experiments.

In the lab, you want your results to be as accurate as possible. Repeating your experiments gives you more data. It also helps you better understand your work.

The best scientists repeat their experiments.

21

WHAT WE LEARN FROM TEMPERATURE

Temperature measurements help scientists better understand the world. Engineers, **chemists**, and other scientists all need to measure temperatures.

Engineers need to know how materials will hold up under very high or very low temperatures. Devices such as smartphones could stop working if their battery gets too hot. Plastic chairs could melt if left outdoors in very high summer heat. Engineers choose the right material for the job.

Chemists need to know how materials will react at different temperatures. Some medicines need to be stored at certain temperatures. Otherwise, they may not work. Testing materials at different temperatures can lead to improvements in many areas of science.

GLOSSARY

accurate: Free of mistakes.

chemist: Someone who studies the field of chemistry, the science that deals with the structure and properties of substances and their changes.

clamp: A device that holds parts tightly together.

contaminate: To pollute.

deionized water: Purified water with minerals removed.

equilibrium: A state of balance.

extreme: Either of two opposite conditions very far from each other.

hypothesis: A prediction about the answer to a question.

precise: Very exact.

procedure: A series of steps followed in a set order.

substance: A matter of a particular kind.

thermistor: A temperature sensor used in digital thermometers.

INDEX

WEBSITES

Due to the changing nature of Internet links, PowerKids Press has developed an online list of websites related to the subject of this book. This site is updated regularly. Please use this link to access the list: www.powerkidslinks.com/lls/temperatures